CAROLINE BIRD is a poet and playwright. Her selected poems, *Rookie* (2022), and *The Air Year* (2020) are two of Carcanet's most popular books of the present decade. She won the Forward Prize for Best Collection in 2020, and has been shortlisted for a number of prizes including the T. S. Eliot Prize, the Costa Book Awards, the Ted Hughes Award, the Polari Prize and the Dylan Thomas Prize. She won a Cholmondeley Award in 2023. Her seventh collection, *Ambush at Still Lake*, was published in June 2024.

RACHEL LONG's debut collection, *My Darling from the Lions* (Picador 2020 / Tin House 2021), was shortlisted for the Forward Prize for Best First Collection, the Costa Book Awards and the Sunday Times Young Writer of the Year Award.

Something New

*Alternative poems
for alternative weddings*

Edited by

**CAROLINE BIRD
AND RACHEL LONG**

PICADOR

First published 2025 by Picador
an imprint of Pan Macmillan
The Smithson, 6 Briset Street, London EC1M 5NR
EU representative: Macmillan Publishers Ireland Ltd, 1st Floor,
The Liffey Trust Centre, 117–126 Sheriff Street Upper,
Dublin 1 D01 YC43
Associated companies throughout the world

ISBN 978-1-0350-6917-0

Copyright © Caroline Bird and Rachel Long 2025

The right of Caroline Bird and Rachel Long to be identified as the editors of this work has been asserted in accordance with the Copyright, Designs and Patents Act 1988.

The permissions acknowledgements on pp. 125–132 constitute an extension of this copyright page.

All rights reserved. No part of this publication may be reproduced, stored in a retrieval system, or transmitted, in any form, or by any means (including, without limitation, electronic, mechanical, photocopying, recording or otherwise) without the prior written permission of the publisher.

Pan Macmillan does not have any control over, or any responsibility for, any author or third-party websites (including, without limitation, URLs, emails and QR codes) referred to in or on this book.

1 3 5 7 9 8 6 4 2

A CIP catalogue record for this book is available from the British Library.

Typeset by Palimpsest Book Production Ltd, Falkirk, Stirlingshire
Printed and bound in the UK using 100% Renewable Electricity by
CPI Group (UK) Ltd

This book is sold subject to the condition that it shall not, by way of trade or otherwise, be lent, hired out, or otherwise circulated without the publisher's prior consent in any form of binding or cover other than that in which it is published and without a similar condition including this condition being imposed on the subsequent purchaser. The publisher does not authorize the use or reproduction of any part of this book in any manner for the purpose of training artificial intelligence technologies or systems. The publisher expressly reserves this book from the Text and Data Mining exception in accordance with Article 4(3) of the European Union Digital Single Market Directive 2019/790.

Visit **www.picador.com** to read more about
all our books and to buy them.

Contents

Foreword CAROLINE BIRD & RACHEL LONG – ix
Small Wedding DOROTHY MOLLOY – 1
Traditional Virgin Islands Wedding Verse TIPHANIE YANIQUE – 2
Looking at Each Other MURIEL RUKEYSER – 4
The Kiss ANNE SEXTON – 5
For What Binds Us JANE HIRSHFIELD – 6
Love Poem with Apologies for My Appearance ADA LIMÓN – 7
We Two Boys Together Clinging WALT WHITMAN – 8
Serenade TERRANCE HAYES – 9
Scaffolding SEAMUS HEANEY – 11
Vow CLARE SHAW – 12
A Prayer at Squire Street, 2009 KEI MILLER – 15
Love KAE TEMPEST – 16
Measuring Light THERESA LOLA – 17
The Wedding Vow SHARON OLDS – 19
The Owl and the Pussy-Cat EDWARD LEAR – 21
From the Irish IAN DUHIG – 23
Nigh-No-Place JEN HADFIELD – 24
Megan Married Herself CAROLINE BIRD – 26
Having a Coke with You FRANK O'HARA – 28
For Days Now I Have Been Imagining It SELIMA HILL – 30
Obsessive Cannibal Love Poem MICHAEL PEDERSEN – 32
The Kiss STEPHEN DUNN – 33
The Stags KATHLEEN JAMIE – 34
Come. And Be My Baby MAYA ANGELOU – 35

Friday Night Drift JAKE HAWKEY – 36
Habitation MARGARET ATWOOD – 38
I want to get high my whole life with you HERA LINDSAY BIRD – 39
Gold DONALD HALL – 41
As If RACHEL LONG – 42
i love you to the moon & CHEN CHEN – 43
Watch Us Laugh as We Gather ROGER ROBINSON – 44
A Lang Promise JACKIE KAY – 45
That's My Heart Right There WILLIE PERDOMO – 46
Epithalamium NICK LAIRD – 47
Variations on the Word Love MARGARET ATWOOD – 48
A Boy Gets Married LEWIS BUXTON – 50
What I Didn't Know Before ADA LIMÓN – 51
American Wedding ESSEX HEMPHILL – 52
The Weight LINDA GREGG – 54
San Antonio NAOMI SHIHAB NYE – 55
The Lovers TIMOTHY LIU – 56
The Wedding Dress SELIMA HILL – 57
Short Talk on the Sensation of Airplane Takeoff ANNE CARSON – 57
Contingency ANDREA COHEN – 57
Promise MAGGIE NELSON – 58
Eternity Ring DOROTHY MOLLOY – 59
[It's no use / Mother dear . . .] SAPPHO – 60
In Another Life KIM MOORE – 61
Cat Worship GOLNOOSH NOUR – 62
Like That KIM ADDONIZIO – 63
White Writing CAROL ANN DUFFY – 65

Cornucopia NATASHA RAO – 66

One Hundred Love Sonnets: XVII PABLO NERUDA – 67

Romantic STEPHEN SEXTON – 68

Sonnet XXX: 'Love is not all' EDNA ST VINCENT MILLAY – 69

A Declaration of Need JOHN HEGLEY – 70

The Shape of Her CHRISTINA DUNHILL – 71

Love Poem HELEN MORT – 73

Pride's Crossing JAMES TATE – 74

First Thought after Seeing You Smile WARSAN SHIRE – 75

I Married You LINDA PASTAN – 76

Waiting RAYMOND CARVER – 77

I Don't Want to Live a Small Life MARY OLIVER – 78

Bridled Vows IAN DUHIG – 79

For the New House URSULA K. LE GUIN – 80

I Wanna Be Yours JOHN COOPER CLARKE – 81

Poem DENIS JOHNSON – 82

Marriage Song TONY HOAGLAND – 83

For Keeps JOY HARJO – 85

Romantic Comedy LORRAINE MARINER – 86

O Small Sad Ecstasy of Love ANNE CARSON – 87

When I hear your name GLORIA FUERTES – 88

Science DAN RHODES – 90

7301 U. A. FANTHORPE – 91

Honeymooners' Ghazal KATHRYN BEVIS – 92

'It was as if I were asleep' EMILY BERRY – 93

Transformation ADAM ZAGAJEWSKI – 94

When You Are Near, I Turn into a
Baja Fairy Duster AIMEE NEZHUKUMATATHIL – 95

The Year We Married Birds LIZ BERRY – 96
Wedding Weather LEONTIA FLYNN – 98
blessing the boats LUCILLE CLIFTON – 99
from Twenty-One Love Poems ADRIENNE RICH – 100
Saying Something CAROL ANN DUFFY – 101
The Present MICHAEL DONAGHY – 102
in your kitchen KATIE O'PRAY – 103
I promise when I lift your egg JACK UNDERWOOD – 104
This One's for You RACHEL LONG – 105
Pull Out All the Stops ANTHONY VAHNI CAPILDEO – 106
'Let me put it this way' SIMON ARMITAGE – 108
One Enchanted Evening DARA WIER – 109
Honeymoon at Weybourne LUKE WRIGHT – 110
Wife JANE CLARKE – 111
The Amnesty CAROLINE BIRD – 112
True Love WISŁAWA SZYMBORSKA – 113
I Remember ANNE SEXTON – 115
Two Lighthouses JULIA DARLING – 116
Prayer for a Marriage STEVE SCAFIDI – 117
Sonnets from the Portuguese XIV:
'If thou must love me' ELIZABETH BARRETT BROWNING – 118
Mountain Dew Commercial Disguised
as a Love Poem MATTHEW OLZMANN – 119
The Dereliction LIZ BERRY – 121
I Loved You Before I Was Born LI-YOUNG LEE – 122

Acknowledgements – 124
Copyright Acknowledgements – 125

Foreword

Why do weddings need poems? Poetry can express the inexpressible, translate longing into language, throw a can of paint over an abstract feeling. We reach for poems on these days because 'love' is too small a syllable to elaborate on the endless uniqueness of the heart. And yet, when asked to read a poem at a wedding, what do we all do, poets included? Google. Frantically.

Even though we want to express something deeply personal, the word 'wedding' can make us panic and reach for stock texts. Understandably, since up until very recently, a wedding was no place for reinvention. Now, gay marriage is legal in Britain; heterosexual couples can have civil partnerships; we can get married in a yurt or a cave or on a rollercoaster. But the old traditions die hard, and despite these apparent new freedoms, the word 'wedding' still holds so many connotations, controlling our imaginations in ways that can feel alienating or limiting; and when it comes to the 'wedding poem' even a *Star Trek* themed do, with guests in skull-caps, will *still* find us translating the same old Shakespeare sonnet into Klingoni.

This anthology aims to shake that up, featuring poems you won't find on many 'lists' in your desperate Google search. Alternative poems for alternative weddings, be they small, huge, camp as Christmas, hilarious, glamorous, shot-gun, a third wedding held in a nursing home, or the low-key but profound culmination of a forty-year love. Bored of these 'one size fits all' wedding poems, we have curated one hundred and one newly selected poems for the big day – of all sizes, flavours and styles – so you can properly personalise your choice. Some are cheeky, some are weird, sexy, subtle, domestic, ecstatic and sweet. Every couple is different, so rather than creating a safe generic tone across the whole book, we've tried to include *all* tones, so that something – even just one poem – will speak to your wedding specifically; and if a poem speaks *to* you, it will speak *like* you. Also, you have our permission to edit on the day. If you love a poem and yet one line isn't quite right for your shindig, cut it out! The poet will forgive you.

And if you're not getting married or attending a wedding, but simply fancied reading a collection of love poetry – welcome. We want it to be enjoyed as a book in itself, as a celebration of the multiplicity of love, and the risky, glorious human desire to make a promise to the future.

Caroline Bird
Rachel Long

Something New

Small Wedding

They wanted a small wedding. Found a priest
who did it for a song. They gave each other
barmbrack rings; a pea, a bean, a stick, a rag;
a Christmas cracker joke, a paper-hat.

He wore a pin-striped suit with wide lapels
and ankle flares. She wore her polka-dots.

Her bouquet was a dandelion; his buttonhole
a daisy; the wedding breakfast, ice-cream
on a doily with a peach.

Jenny moved a mountain just to be there.
Stephen made a speech.

DOROTHY MOLLOY

Traditional Virgin Islands Wedding Verse

for Hannah and James

When you are born
you are passed to your father's arms
or your mother's chest.
Your parents claim you. You belong
to them. Before you even know
you are your own,
you know that you are
someone else's. You are
bonded. You need to belong.

Then you belong
to the land, the town
in which you are raised. You belong
to the city you choose.
These places have a hold
on you. They claim you.
I am from, you say.
I am of.

Perhaps you belong
to the school. To the church.
You say I am, and name
what you do for sustenance.
These things own you and
you own them.

You are part of a tribe.
It is not a shackle. It is the true story
of self-creation.

It is what makes you.
You come to belong to yourself.
You say I am
and call your own name.

And now
you belong
to each other.
You are of the same tribe.
I am his wife,
you will say; and
I am her husband.
You are future ancestors of
the same village.

And you have made this so
by your own choice.

You will weld yourself
with regard to each other
and because of each other.
You will weave your own self
to the other. You are now native
to each other. You say
I am
yours.
I claim you.

TIPHANIE YANIQUE

Looking at Each Other

Yes, we were looking at each other
Yes, we knew each other very well
Yes, we had made love with each other many times
Yes, we had heard music together
Yes, we had gone to the sea together
Yes, we had cooked and eaten together
Yes, we had laughed often day and night
Yes, we fought violence and knew violence
Yes, we hated the inner and outer oppression
Yes, that day we were looking at each other
Yes, we saw the sunlight pouring down
Yes, the corner of the table was between us
Yes, bread and flowers were on the table
Yes, our eyes saw each other's eyes
Yes, our mouths saw each other's mouths
Yes, our breasts saw each other's breasts
Yes, our bodies entire saw each other
Yes, it was beginning in each
Yes, it threw waves across our lives
Yes, the pulses were becoming very strong
Yes, the beating became very delicate
Yes, the calling   the arousal
Yes, the arriving   the coming
Yes, there it was for both entire
Yes, we were looking at each other

MURIEL RUKEYSER

The Kiss

My mouth blooms like a cut.
I've been wronged all year, tedious
nights, nothing but rough elbows in them
and delicate boxes of Kleenex calling *crybaby
crybaby, you fool!*

Before today my body was useless.
Now it's tearing at its square corners.
It's tearing old Mary's garments off, knot by knot
and see – Now it's shot full of these electric bolts.
Zing! A resurrection!

Once it was a boat, quite wooden
and with no business, no salt water under it
and in need of some paint. It was no more
than a group of boards. But you hoisted her, rigged her.
She's been elected.

My nerves are turned on. I hear them like
musical instruments. Where there was silence
the drums, the strings are incurably playing. You did this.
Pure genius at work. Darling, the composer has stepped
into fire.

ANNE SEXTON

For What Binds Us

There are names for what binds us:
strong forces, weak forces.
Look around, you can see them:
the skin that forms in a half-empty cup,
nails rusting into the places they join,
joints dovetailed on their own weight.
The way things stay so solidly
wherever they've been set down –
and gravity, scientists say, is weak.

And see how the flesh grows back
across a wound, with a great vehemence,
more strong
than the simple, untested surface before.
There's a name for it on horses,
when it comes back darker and raised: proud flesh,

as all flesh,
is proud of its wounds, wears them
as honors given out after battle,
small triumphs pinned to the chest –

And when two people have loved each other
see how it is like a
scar between their bodies,
stronger, darker, and proud;
how the black cord makes of them a single fabric
that nothing can tear or mend.

JANE HIRSHFIELD

Love Poem with Apologies for My Appearance

Sometimes, I think you get the worst
of me. The much-loved loose forest green
sweat pants, the long bra-less days, hair
knotted and uncivilized, a shadowed brow
where the devilish thoughts do their hoofed
dance on the brain. I'd like to say this means
I love you, the stained white cotton T-shirt,
the tears, pistachio shells, the mess of orange
peels on my desk, but it's different than that.
I move in this house with you, the way I move
in my mind, unencumbered by beauty's cage.
I do like I do in the tall grass, more animal-me
than much else. I'm wrong, it is that I love you,
but it's more that when you say it back, lights
out, a cold wind through curtains, for maybe
the first time in my life, I believe it.

ADA LIMÓN

We Two Boys Together Clinging

We two boys together clinging,
One the other never leaving,
Up and down the roads going, North and South excursions making,
Power enjoying, elbows stretching, fingers clutching,
Armed and fearless, eating, drinking, sleeping, loving,
No law less than ourselves owning, sailing, soldiering, thieving, threatening,
Misers, menials, priests alarming, air breathing, water drinking, on the turf or the sea-beach dancing,
Cities wrenching, ease scorning, statues mocking, feebleness chasing,
Fulfilling our foray.

WALT WHITMAN

Serenade

I want to always sleep beneath a bright red blanket
of leaves. I want to never wear a coat of ice.
I want to learn to walk without blinking.
I want to learn the language of a Chilean poet.
I want to say God & fuck you & touch me
without blinking. I want to outlive the turtle
& the turtle's father, the stone. I want a mouth
full of permissions & a pink glistening bud.
If the wildflower & ant hill can return
after sleeping three seasons, I want to walk
out of this house wearing nothing but wind.
I want to greet you, I want to wait for the bus with you
weighing less than a chill. I want to fight off the bolts
of gray lighting the alcoves & winding paths
of your hair. I want to fight off the damp nudgings
of snow. I want to fight off the wind.
I want to be the wind & I want to fight off the wind
with its sagging banner of isolation, its swinging
screen doors, its gilded boxes, & neatly folded pamphlets
of noise. I want to fight off the dull straight lines
of two by fours & endings, your disapprovals,
your doubts & regulations, your carbon copies.
If the locust can abandon its suit,
I want a brand new name. I want the pepper's fury
& the salt's tenderness. I want the eight-sided passion
of sugar, but not its need. I want the virtue
of the evening rain, but not its gossip.
I want the moon's intuition, but not its questions.
I want the malice of nothing on earth. I want to enter
every room in a strange electrified city
& find you there. I want your lips around the bell of flesh

at the bottom of my ear. I want to be the mirror,
but not the nightstand. I do not want to be the light switch.
I do not want to be the yellow photograph
or book of poems. When I leave this body, Woman,
I want to be pure flame and song. I want to be your breath.

TERRANCE HAYES

Scaffolding

Masons, when they start upon a building,
Are careful to test out the scaffolding;
Make sure that planks won't slip at busy points,
Secure all ladders, tighten bolted joints.
And yet all this comes down when the job's done
Showing off walls of sure and solid stone.
So if, my dear, there sometimes seem to be
Old bridges breaking between you and me
Never fear. We may let the scaffolds fall
Confident that we have built our wall.

SEAMUS HEANEY

Vow

Say yes.
That word on your lips
is a kiss;
is a promise already made.
We made it.

Love did not turn from hurt
or hard work.
When lights failed, it did not switch off.
When love had no road,
we willingly built it.

We shouldered its stones
and its dirt. So thank god
there are days like this when it's easy.
When we open our mouths
and the words flood in.

Put the word of your hand
in mine.
We have learnt to hold to each other
when nothing was given by right;
how love will insist
with its ache; with its first painful
tug on the guts;

its snake in the nest of the ribs;
the bomb in the chest;
in the Y of the thighs; the red, red
red sun of it, rising.
How love must, at all costs,

be answered. We have answered
and so have a million before us
and each of their names is a vow.
So now I can tell you, quite simply
you are the house I will live in:

there is no good reason
to move. Good earth,
you are home, stone, sun,
all my countries. Vital to me
as the light. You are it

and I am asking.
Say yes.

Love opens a door
then slams it. It does.
It loses its touch and its looks.
But love needs its fury.
We have fought

and when times make it necessary,
we will again. When night draws in,
we won't forget
how once the streets ran wet with light
and love. Like blood. They will again.

But for now,
we make our promises gently.
This extraordinary day we have made.
Listen –
the birds in their ordinary heaven.

Tonight the sky will blaze
with stars. Today, my love,
rooms bloom with flowers.
Say yes.
The sky is ours.

                CLARE SHAW

A Prayer at Squire Street, 2009

Bless this home that we have bought –
each corner, each window, the high
and slanting roof; bless the colour
of our rooms, and then bless the rooms
that shall know us better than we know ourselves.
Bless the stairs that our door opens to,
may we always ascend into our home
in peace.
This used to be a church, so blessings should come
easy. Now bless our bed, the first
we have bought together;
bless its board and its sponge.
May we never grow weary of love.

KEI MILLER

Love

The way you hold your cup in a closed fist
Your wrists that get rheumatic in the rain
Your long feet, long legs and bony shoulders
Your smile a crash of teeth from nose to chin.

Your eyes drop three octaves when you want me
Your body is transposed into the key
Of sand dunes, raw quartz, heat from a slow sun.
Suddenly as graceful as when you dance
No longer smashing your limbs into
Unmoving table-tops or burning your hands
On every available hot surface
Or head-butting the car door when you dive in

You know, it used to keep me up at night,
The lack of you

KAE TEMPEST

Measuring Light

All that paperwork, legal uniformity.
We swim in the pale pool of history.

We joke that he could have taken mine.
Either way someone surrenders.

I always liked the sound of his surname –
perhaps it was just instinctive.

My husband and I have now reached
for the physics of being

to find a resolution we can rest in.
We stand before each other,

our faces appear transfigured.
We unveil each other in unison.

By sharing one surname,
we declare we have combined

our individual lights.
We call it concentrated radiance.

A letter has come in
addressed to Mr & Mrs –

I smile, & light, so much of it, pours out
of my body, to the table, floor,

even flows out from under the door.
This pool is glistening.

I see it, know it, feel it.
We swim in it.

THERESA LOLA

The Wedding Vow

I did not stand at the altar, I stood
at the foot of the chancel steps, with my beloved,
and the minister stood on the top step
holding the open Bible. The church
was wood, painted ivory inside, no people – God's
stable perfectly cleaned. It was night,
spring – outside, a moat of mud,
and inside, from the rafters, flies
fell onto the open Bible, and the minister
tilted it and brushed them off. We stood
beside each other, crying slightly
with fear and awe. In truth, we had married
that first night, in bed, we had been
married by our bodies, but now we stood
in history – what our bodies had said,
mouth to mouth, we now said publicly,
gathered together, death. We stood
holding each other by the hand, yet I also
stood as if alone, for a moment,
just before the vow, though taken
years before, took. It was a vow
of the present and the future, and yet I felt it
to have some touch on the distant past
or the distant past on it, I felt
the silent, dry, crying ghost of my
parents' marriage there, somewhere
in the bright space – perhaps one of the
plummeting flies, bouncing slightly
as it hit forsaking all others, then was brushed
away. I felt as if I had come
to claim a promise – the sweetness I'd inferred

from their sourness; and at the same time that I had
come, congenitally unworthy, to beg.
And yet, I had been working toward this hour
all my life. And then it was time
to speak – he was offering me, no matter
what, his life. That is all I had to
do, that evening, to accept the gift
I had longed for – to say I had accepted it,
as if being asked if I breathe. Do I take?
I do. I take as he takes – we have been
practising this. Do you bear this pleasure? I do.

SHARON OLDS

The Owl and the Pussy-Cat

I

The Owl and the Pussy-cat went to sea
   In a beautiful pea-green boat,
They took some honey, and plenty of money,
   Wrapped up in a five-pound note.
The Owl looked up to the stars above,
   And sang to a small guitar,
"O lovely Pussy! O Pussy, my love,
   What a beautiful Pussy you are,
      You are,
      You are!
What a beautiful Pussy you are!"

II

Pussy said to the Owl, "You elegant fowl!
   How charmingly sweet you sing!
O let us be married! too long we have tarried:
   But what shall we do for a ring?"
They sailed away, for a year and a day,
   To the land where the Bong-Tree grows
And there in a wood a Piggy-wig stood
   With a ring at the end of his nose,
      His nose,
      His nose,
   With a ring at the end of his nose.

III

"Dear Pig, are you willing to sell for one shilling
  Your ring?" Said the Piggy, "I will."
So they took it away, and were married next day
  By the Turkey who lives on the hill.
They dined on mince, and slices of quince,
  Which they ate with a runcible spoon;
And hand in hand, on the edge of the sand,
  They danced by the light of the moon,
    The moon,
    The moon,
They danced by the light of the moon.

EDWARD LEAR

From the Irish

According to Dinneen, a Gael unsurpassed
in lexicographical enterprise, the Irish
for moon means 'the white circle in a slice
of half-boiled potato or turnip'. A star
is the mark on the forehead of the beast
and the sun is the bottom of a lake, or well.

Well, if I say to you your face
is like a slice of half-boiled turnip,
your hair is the colour of a lake's bottom
and at the centre of each of your eyes
is the mark of the beast, it is because
I want to love you properly, according to Dinneen.

IAN DUHIG

Nigh-No-Place

I prithee, let me bring thee where crabs grow;
And I with my long nails will dig thee pignuts . . .
  – The Tempest

I will meet you at Pity Me Wood.
I will meet you at Up-To-No-Good.

I will meet you at Stank, Shank and Stye.
I will meet you at Blowfly.

I will meet you at Low Spying How.
I will meet you at Salt Pie.

I will meet you at Coppertop.
I will meet you at Scandale Bottom.

I will meet you at Crackpot Moor
I will meet you at Muker.

I will meet you at Dirty Piece.
I will meet you at Booze, Alberta.

I will meet you at Bloody Vale.
I will meet you at Hunger Hill.

I will bring you to New Invention.
I will bring you to Lucky Seven.

I will bring you from Shivery Man.
I will bring you to The Lion and Lamb.

I will bring you to the North Light.
I will bring you to Quiet-the-Night.

I will bring you to Hush.
I will bring you to Hungry Hushes.

I will bring you to Grace, Alberta.
I will bring you to Nigh-No-Place.

I will meet you at Two O'Clock Creek.
Will you go with me?

     JEN HADFIELD

Megan Married Herself

She arrived at the country mansion in a silver limousine.
She'd sent out invitations and everything:
her name written twice with '&' in the middle,
the calligraphy of coupling.
She strode down the aisle to 'At Last' by Etta James,
faced the celebrant like a keen soldier reporting for duty,
her voice shaky yet sure. I do. I do.
"You may now kiss the mirror." Applause. Confetti.
Every single one of the hundred and forty guests
deemed the service 'unimprovable.'
Especially the vows. So 'from the heart.'
Her wedding gown was ivory; pointedly off-white,
"After all, we've shared a bed for thirty-two years,"
she quipped in her first speech,
"I'm hardly virginal if you know what I mean."
(No one knew *exactly* what she meant.)
Not a soul questioned their devotion.
You only had to look at them. Hand cupped in hand.
Smiling out of the same eyes. You could sense
their secret language, bone-deep, blended blood.
Toasts were frequent, tearful. One guest
eyed his wife – hovering harmlessly at the bar – and
imagined what his life might've been if
he'd responded, years ago, to that offer in his head:
"I'm the only one who will ever truly understand you.
Marry me, Derek. I love you. Marry Me."
At the time, he hadn't taken his proposal seriously.
He recharged his champagne flute, watched

the newlywed cut her five-tiered cake, both hands
on the knife. "Is it too late for us to try?" Derek whispered
to no one, as the bride glided herself onto the dance floor,
taking turns first to lead then follow.

CAROLINE BIRD

Having a Coke with You

is even more fun than going to San Sebastian, Irún,
    Hendaye, Biarritz, Bayonne
or being sick to my stomach on the Travesera de Gracia in
    Barcelona
partly because in your orange shirt you look like a better
    happier St Sebastian
partly because of my love for you, partly because of your
    love for yoghurt
partly because of the fluorescent orange tulips around the
    birches
partly because of the secrecy our smiles take on before
    people and statuary
it is hard to believe when I'm with you that there can be
    anything as still
as solemn as unpleasantly definitive as statuary when right
    in front of it
in the warm New York 4 o'clock light we are drifting back
    and forth
between each other like a tree breathing through its spectacles
and the portrait show seems to have no faces in it at all,
    just paint
you suddenly wonder why in the world anyone ever did them
                                                                    I look
at you and I would rather look at you than all the portraits in
    the world
except possibly for the *Polish Rider* occasionally and
    anyway it's in the Frick
which thank heavens you haven't gone to yet so we can go
    together for the first time
and the fact that you move so beautifully more or less takes
    care of Futurism

just as at home I never think of the *Nude Descending a Staircase* or
at a rehearsal a single drawing of Leonardo or Michelangelo that used to wow me
and what good does all the research of the Impressionists do them
when they never got the right person to stand near the tree when the sun sank
or for that matter Marino Marini when he didn't pick the rider as carefully
as the horse
                                      it seems they were all cheated of some marvellous experience
which is not going to go wasted on me which is why I'm telling you about it

FRANK O'HARA

For Days Now I Have Been Imagining It

For days now I have been imagining it:
my taking a deep breath,
my stepping into the room,
your coming slowly towards me
as a lily might –
but what will become of us then,
I want to know:
will it be over?

In spite of our secrets,
as rare and painfully inadequate
as the tadpoles of the forested regions of Borneo;

in spite of our faith,
grim as a mountain range
which we climb and climb,
never to reach the summit,
with its unparalleled views of the surrounding countryside;

in spite of the sheets,
in violet, cerise and mint,
that a nocturnal well-wisher left at the door for us,
will it be over?

And if you think I am going to sit here all afternoon
dreaming about our future,
you're absolutely right:
I'm going to pick you up
like a bridegroom made of sugar on a wedding-cake,
with sugar bones,
and carry you off to the bruised lakes of the future –

with bracelets, cinnamon and shampoo,
we will set up home together on the banks,
just us, and a knee-high moon,
and a few yurts.

SELIMA HILL

Obsessive Cannibal Love Poem

Today is *yes please* and *now* to zipping your
skin around me, to wrapping up in you
like a winter coat with matching scarf
and walking barefoot on powdered snow,
you: the flakes squeezing
between my toes; the biscuits I brought
to snack on are your bones baked
and sweetened; like counting stars
I do not think I will ever be done
kissing you: honey all over
and deep inside, I will swallow
your dancing tongue; take your
daydreams into my nightdreams, all
neu-wave heavenly, ethereal gleam
on wet tarmac, enemy of the rain
which fell between us, which has
no business being there.

Other days a text message
or quick chat on the phone
will do just fine –
I never can tell.

MICHAEL PEDERSEN

The Kiss

She pressed her lips to mind.
— a typo

How many years I must have yearned
for someone's lips against mind.
Pheromones, newly born, were floating
between us. There was hardly any air.

She kissed me again, reaching that place
that sends messages to toes and fingertips,
then all the way to something like home.
Some music was playing on its own.

Nothing like a woman who knows
to kiss the right thing at the right time,
then kisses the things she's missed.
How had I ever settled for less?

I was thinking this is intelligence,
this is the wisest tongue
since the Oracle got into a Greek's ear,
speaking sense. It's the Good,

defining itself. I was out of my mind.
She was in. We married as soon as we could.

STEPHEN DUNN

The Stags

This is the multitude, the beasts
you wanted to show me, drawing me
upstream, all morning up through wind-
scoured heather to the hillcrest.
Below us, in the next glen, is the grave
calm brotherhood, descended
out of winter, out of hunger, kneeling
like the signatories of a covenant;
their weighty, antique-polished antlers
rising above the vegetation
like masts in a harbour, or city spires.
We lie close together, and though the wind
whips away our man-and-woman smell, every
stag-face seems to look toward us, toward,
but not to us: we're held, and hold them,
in civil regard. I suspect you'd
hoped to impress me, to lift to my sight
our shared country, lead me deeper
into what you know, but loath
to cause fear you're already moving
quietly away, sure I'll go with you,
as I would now, almost anywhere.

KATHLEEN JAMIE

Come. And Be My Baby

The highway is full of big cars going nowhere fast
And folks is smoking anything that'll burn
Some people wrap their lives around a cocktail glass
And you sit wondering
Where you're going to turn.
I got it.
Come. And be my baby.

Some prophets say the world is gonna end tomorrow
But others say we've got a week or two
The paper is full of every kind of blooming horror
And you sit wondering
What you're gonna do.
I got it.
Come. And be my baby.

MAYA ANGELOU

Friday Night Drift

You get home & my heart
leaps then rolls like a vast
brass band marching through town

*

The working week has worn you through,
so you sleep lightly in the nook
between my shoulder blade
& the crest of my chest,
raising your head
every now & then to ask,
I can't hear your heartbeat?
Can you help me take my earrings off?

Pinocchio is a real boy thus a liar,
but my love, would I do anything to prevent
damaging your innocent outlook,
even if it meant keeping a secret or two
from you? My love, of course.
Every old ship is surely allowed its secrets.

Would I read poems to our child
while you carried them to term?
My love, of course. Would I fight for you
until a bloody death? Yes, & I would walk the plank . . .

but I'm not explaining the bloody plot again
if you can't keep your droopy eyes open!
O my darling, we've half-watched so many
dramas by now, imagining our own conclusions.

I google the synonyms for acceptance:
receipt, receiving, taking, obtaining, undertaking,
welcoming, embracing, approval, adoption;
I'm surprised by the number of doing words,
I'm surprised acceptance doesn't have any real family.

What was the name of the film we watched
about the landlady who gets married
to the sailor who spoke a great metaphor for love?
I must have been sleeping, you say.
Yes I remember – his sailor friend asks him why he stays
& he surveys the sea before declaring something like,
because I'm just a small, flawed boat in the terrific blue
& when we docked at this port, I liked it here,
they'll say there are better ports but I really like it here

JAKE HAWKEY

Habitation

Marriage is not
a house or even a tent

it is before that, and colder:

the edge of the forest, the edge
of the desert
          the unpainted stairs
at the back where we squat
outside, eating popcorn

the edge of the receding glacier

where painfully and with wonder
at having survived even
this far

we are learning to make fire

        MARGARET ATWOOD

I want to get high my whole life with you

i feel it in my leather hotpant pockets
i feel it in my anime wind blowing through an alpine tennis resort overcome with wildflowers
i feel it in my ironic valley girl hairflip
i feel it in my admittedly limited knowledge of the Roman mythologies
i feel it in my biopic about a corrupt alcoholic educational resource salesman advertising increasingly less and less educational resources
i want to get high my whole life with you
i feel it in my anime wind blowing through an alpine tennis resort overcome with wildflowers AGAIN, and the poem isn't even halfway over yet
so what if my blood is the wind
so what if I love you so much I am becoming stupid
my heart melting like red candles on Satan's birthday cake

i want to get high with you at an industrial carpet outlet store
i want to get high with you at the top of the Grand Canyon and pretend like you are going to push me into and scream and pretend to try not to get pushed in even though i know you pushing me in is the last thing you want because if you did that i'd die and you don't want me to die
i love you so much i tell you about it
i love you so much i have already picked out my grave and written your name on it
when you laugh in the dark
it fills up the corners of the room with a thousand upside-down cartoon bats

how dare you be the kind of person I would immediately fall
    completely in
love with and be devastated if you left
how dare you come and do that
your eyes
like two black cats
licking their assholes
in the hot morning sun of my face

O this feeling has drenched my bones
and turned my skeleton pink
with you i feel my mind changing
with you i feel my blood changing
i want to get really good at woodwork...........

....

I want to get really good at woodwork
and go into the forest
and cut up some logs
and make you a beautiful house to live in

HERA LINDSAY BIRD

Gold

Pale gold of the walls, gold
of the centers of daisies, yellow roses
pressing from a clear bowl. All day
we lay on the bed, my hand
stroking the deep
gold of your thighs and your back.
We slept and woke
entering the golden room together,
lay down in it breathing
quickly, then
slowly again,
caressing and dozing, your hand sleepily
touching my hair now.

We made in those days
tiny identical rooms inside our bodies
which the men who uncover our graves
will find in a thousand years,
shining and whole.

DONALD HALL

As If

Earlier, I missed you in the honey aisle. I want
to be en pointe in the kitchen, open the highest cupboard,
set the things you like inside; white bread, long-life cow's milk,
I even bought instant coffee
and refrained from informing the cashier
that it wasn't for me, woman of refined taste.
Who am I kidding? I'd buy a sack of rice
and lug it back on my head. I don't even hate admitting this,
I've forgotten what I once did, before I glowed
in search of slippers. If you don't like your feet touching the
   floor,
they don't have to anymore.

RACHEL LONG

i love you to the moon &

not back, let's not come back, let's go by the speed of
queer zest & stay up
there & get ourselves a little
moon cottage (so pretty), then start a moon garden

with lots of moon veggies (so healthy), i mean
i was already moonlighting
as an online moonologist
most weekends, so this is the immensely

logical next step, are you
packing your bags yet, don't forget your
sailor moon jean jacket, let's wear
our sailor moon jean jackets while twirling in that lighter,

queerer moon gravity, let's love each other
(so good) on the moon, let's love
the moon
on the moon

CHEN CHEN

Watch Us Laugh as We Gather

For Nicola

And if you raise your voice
in song, I'll catch the chorus,
back you up, hum along.
No one's called me a singer,
but watch me sing for you.
Sing this tune through a throat
that's hoarse no matter, and my pitch
is off no matter, sing when we've won,
sing when we've lost
and laugh as we gather. Our bellies
bulging with breath as we stretch
our throats to cool blue skies.
So this life gave us tough songs
to sing, so why not wring those notes
through our pink rubber tongues.
I'm right beside you, singing strong,
singing even if I don't know the song.

ROGER ROBINSON

A Lang Promise

Whether the weather be dreich or fair, my luve,
if guid times greet us, or we hae tae face the worst,
ahint and afore whit will happen tae us:
blind in the present, eyes open to the furore,
unkempt or perjink, suddenly puir or poorly,
peely-wally or in fine fettle, beld or frosty,
calm as a ghoul or in a feery-farry,
in dork December or in springy spring weather,
doon by the Barrows, on the Champs-Élysées,
at midnicht, first licht, whether the mune
be roond or crescent, and yer o' soond mind
or absent, I'll tak your trusty haun
and lead you over the haw – hame, ma darlin.
I'll carry ma lantern, and daur defend ye agin ony foe;
and whilst there is breath in me, I'll blaw it intae ye.
Fir ye are ma true luve, the bonnie face I see;
nichts I fall intae slumber, it's ye swimming up
in all yer guidness and blitheness, yer passion.
You'll be mine, noo, an' till the end o' time,
ma bonnie lassie, I'll tak the full guid o' ye'
and gie it back, and gie it back tae ye:
a furst kiss, a lang promise, time's gowden ring.

JACKIE KAY

That's My Heart Right There

We used to say,
That's my heart right there.

As if to say,
Don't mess with her right there.

As if, don't even play,
That's a part of me right there.

In other words, okay okay,
That's the start of me right there.

As if, come that day,
That's the end of me right there.

As if, push come to shove,
I would fend for her right there.

As if, come what may,
I would lie for her right there.

As if, come love to pay,
I would die for that right there.

WILLIE PERDOMO

Epithalamium

You're beeswax and I'm birdshit.
I'm mostly harmless. You're irrational.
If I'm iniquity then you're theft.
One of us is supercalifragilistic.

If I'm the most insane disgusting filth
you're hardly curiosa.
You're bubblewrap to my fingertips.
You're winter sleep and I'm the bee dance.

And I am menthol and you are eggshell.
When you're atrocious I am Spellcheck.
You're the yen. I'm the Nepalese pound.
If I'm homesteading you're radical chic.

I'm carpet shock and you're the rail.
I'm Memory Foam Day on Price-Drop TV
and you're the Lord of Misrule who shrieks
when I surface in goggles through duckweed,

and I am Trafalgar, and you're Waterloo,
and frequently it seems to me that I am you,
and you are me. If I'm the rising incantation
you're the charm, or I am, or you are.

NICK LAIRD

Variations on the Word Love

This is a word we use to plug
holes with. It's the right size for those warm
blanks in speech, for those red heart-
shaped vacancies on the page that look nothing
like real hearts. Add lace
and you can sell
it. We insert it also in the one empty
space on the printed form
that comes with no instructions. There are whole
magazines with not much in them
but the word love, you can
rub it all over your body and you
can cook with it too. How do we know
it isn't what goes on at the cool
debaucheries of slugs under damp
pieces of cardboard? As for the weed-
seedlings nosing their tough snouts up
among the lettuces, they shout it.
Love! Love! sing the soldiers, raising
their glittering knives in salute.

Then there's the two
of us. This word
is far too short for us, it has only
four letters, too sparse
to fill those deep bare
vacuums between the stars
that press on us with their deafness.
It's not love we don't wish
to fall into, but that fear.
This word is not enough but it will

have to do. It's a single
vowel in this metallic
silence, a mouth that says
O again and again in wonder
and pain, a breath, a finger
grip on a cliffside. You can
hold on or let go.

MARGARET ATWOOD

A Boy Gets Married

and the wedding is beautiful, the cake incredible. He glows at the centre of it all in a red dress & sexy garter. At his side is his father, giving him away, his mother crying in the pew. The priest doesn't know what to do with this boyish face at the altar so just gets on with it. It is a fairy tale, a pumpkin for a carriage, but he knew this would be a different kind of marriage: less silk & lace more heather and thistle, no white dress, more arterial. Find him in the forest: something cold, something true, something foraged, something new.

LEWIS BUXTON

What I Didn't Know Before

was how horses simply give birth to other
horses. Not a baby by any means, not
a creature of liminal spaces, but already
a four-legged beast hellbent on walking,
scrambling after the mother. A horse gives way
to another horse and then suddenly there are
two horses, just like that. That's how I loved you.
You, off the long train from Red Bank carrying
a coffee as big as your arm, a bag with two
computers swinging in it unwieldly at your
side. I remember we broke into laughter
when we saw each other. What was between
us wasn't a fragile thing to be coddled, cooed
over. It came out fully formed, ready to run.

ADA LIMÓN

American Wedding

In America,
I place my ring
on your cock
where it belongs.
No horsemen
bearing terror,
no soldiers of doom
will swoop in
and sweep us apart.
They're too busy
looting the land
to watch us.
They don't know
we need each other
critically.
They expect us to call in sick,
watch television all night,
die by our own hands.
They don't know
we are becoming powerful.
Every time we kiss
we confirm the new world coming.

What the rose whispers
before blooming
I vow to you.
I give you my heart,
a safe house.
I give you promises other than
milk, honey, liberty.
I assume you will always

be a free man with a dream.
In America,
place your ring
on my cock
where it belongs.
Long may we live
to free this dream.

ESSEX HEMPHILL

The Weight

Two horses were put together in the same paddock.
Night and day. In the night and in the day
wet from heat and the chill of the wind
on it. Muzzle to water, snorting, head swinging
and the taste of bay in the shadowed air.
The dignity of being. They slept that way
knowing each other always.
Withers quivering for a moment,
fetlock and the proud rise at the base of the tail,
width of back. The volume of them, and each other's weight.
Fences were nothing compared to that.
People were nothing. They slept standing,
their throats curved against the other's rump.
They breathed against each other,
whinnied and stomped.
There are things they did that I do not know.
The privacy of them had a river in it.
Had our universe in it. And the way
its border looks back at us with its light.
This was finally their freedom.
The freedom an oak tree knows.
That is built at night by stars.

LINDA GREGG

San Antonio

Tonight I lingered over your name,
the delicate assembly of vowels
a voice inside my head.
You were sleeping when I arrived.
I stood by your bed
and watched the sheets rise gently.
I knew what slant of light
would make you turn over.
It was then I felt
the highways slide out of my hands.
I remembered the old men
in the west side cafe,
dealing dominoes like magical charms.
It was then I knew,
like a woman looking backward,
I could not leave you,
or find anyone I loved more.

NAOMI SHIHAB NYE

The Lovers

I was always afraid
of the next card

the psychic would turn
over for us –
                    Forgive me
for not knowing
how we were

every card in the deck.

TIMOTHY LIU

The Wedding Dress

The wedding-dress is going Don't ask me!
I don't know what she's doing either!

SELIMA HILL

Short Talk on the Sensation of Airplane Takeoff

Well you know I wonder, it could be love
running towards my life with its arms up
yelling let's buy it what a bargain!

ANNE CARSON

Contingency

In another
life, I'd
want this one.

ANDREA COHEN

Promise

You promise me nothing

I distract myself from this fact
by wondering about the etymology

of promise, promise myself
to look it up later

For now there is a home here

In this bent head
This hand in hair

          MAGGIE NELSON

Eternity Ring

I can't get this blasted thing off:
the ring set with stones that eats into

my flesh. I've tried fretsaws and slashers
and pneumatic drills; Fatima,

butter and soap. Lard.
I rode a tank over my knuckles,

I dropped a bomb onto my hand.
The ring is still grand.

DOROTHY MOLLOY

[It's no use / Mother dear . . .]

It's no use

Mother dear, I
can't finish my
weaving

You may

blame Aphrodite

soft as she is

she has almost
killed me with
love for that boy

SAPPHO, TRANSLATED BY MARY BARNARD

In Another Life

for Jan Glas

I think that in another life, I must have known you –
maybe we were brothers who loved or hated one another
or maybe we were neighbours destined to grow old together
or strangers who nod hello when passing in the street
or maybe one of us was a king, and the other in the army
and on a routine inspection our eyes just met
or maybe we were soldiers who would die for one another,
maybe we were the last two speakers of a minority language,
maybe I was a farm animal and you were a fair-haired farmhand,
maybe we ran away to America together, or maybe we
were miners and loved our yellow canaries, maybe you
were the canary and I felt your heart beating on my palm,
maybe you were a nurse and I was your favourite patient,
maybe we were buried on a hill, standing side by side.

KIM MOORE

Cat Worship

A beautiful woman has a curtain of flesh
    – Persian proverb

You & I are two fat cats in love
two voluptuous women
perhaps obese by cinematic standards
'unhealthy' by our mothers' concerns
only fleshy according to friends.
I cannot imagine myself alive
without your curtain of flesh.
I hide behind it like a shy child when
the world shouts at me, I shelter in your flesh
from pretty much everyone else:
the rich, them straights & the police
I too am a fat feline, terrified & disgusted by pigs.
You walk like a kindly matriarch, no trace of
hesitance in your small feet
your strength knows no shame
your long lashes are thorns in the eyes of envy
your crown of hair shines in the sun & rain
your power bejewelled by compassion
you cleanse the air with your soft breath
you beautify the sunlight with your manicured claws
you wave your scarlet nails in the air like a disdainful
diva, when I'm upset by pettiness, when I'm bruised & sick
paranoid – for the right reasons – at times even insane,
my only cure to be as close as possible:
warm velvet, my beatific shelter,
the only promise I cannot break.

GOLNOOSH NOUR

Like That

Love me like a wrong turn on a bad road late at night, with
    no moon and no town anywhere
and a large hungry animal moving heavily through the brush
    in the ditch.
Love me with a blindfold over your eyes and the sound of
    rusty water
blurting from the faucet in the kitchen, leaking down through
the floorboards to hot cement. Do it without asking,
without wondering or thinking anything, while the machinery's
shut down and the watchman's slumped asleep before his
    small TV
showing the empty garage, the deserted hallways, while the
    thieves slice
through the fence with steel clippers. Love me when you
    can't find
a decent restaurant open anywhere, when you're alone in a
    glaring diner
with two nuns arguing in the back booth, when your eggs
    are greasy
and your hash browns underdone. Snick the buttons off the
    front of my dress
and toss them one by one into the pond where carp lurk
    just beneath the surface,
their cold fins waving. Love me on the hood of a truck no
    one's driven
in years, sunk to its fenders in weeds and dead sunflowers;
and in the lilies, your mouth on my white throat, while
    turtles drag
their bellies through slick mud, through the footprints of
    coots and ducks.

Do it when no one's looking, when the riots begin and the planes
open up, when the bus leaps the curb and the driver hits the brakes and the
pedal sinks to the floor, while someone hurls a plate against the wall
and picks up another, love me like a freezing shot of vodka, like pure agave,
love me when you're lonely, when we're both too tired to speak, when you
don't believe in anything, listen, there isn't anything, it doesn't matter;
lie down with me and close your eyes, the road curves here, I'm cranking up
the radio and we're going, we won't turn back as long as you love me,
as long as you keep on doing it exactly like that.

KIM ADDONIZIO

White Writing

No vows written to wed you,
I write them white,
my lips on yours,
light in the soft hours of our married years.

No prayers written to bless you,
I write them white,
your soul a flame,
bright in the window of your maiden name.

No laws written to guard you,
I write them white,
your hand in mine,
palm against palm, lifeline, heartline.

No rules written to guide you,
I write them white,
words on the wind,
traced with a stick where we walk on the sand.

No news written to tell you,
I write it white,
foam on a wave
as we lift up our skirts in the sea, wade,

see last gold sun behind clouds,
inked water in moonlight.
No poems written to praise you,
I write them white.

CAROL ANN DUFFY

Cornucopia

Morning after we meet: a parade
in the street. Brass instruments blasting

gladly. Of the dozen we crack,
ten eggs hold double yolks.

When it rains, the town floods. Your dog
and your neighbors huddle at the window.

Suddenly: our dog, our neighbors.
Our basement, puddled.

Mouse poop like cartoon jewels
glittering inside the white shoe.

Millions of seeds arrow upward into green.
Your legs entwine mine in earthworm parody.

Inside each day, I can feel the round outline
of all the time in the world.

The fruit bowl overflows. Tiny flies
multiply.

NATASHA RAO

One Hundred Love Sonnets: XVII

I don't love you as if you were a rose of salt, topaz,
or arrow of carnations that propagate fire:
I love you as one loves certain obscure things,
secretly, between the shadow and the soul.

I love you as the plant that doesn't bloom but carries
the light of those flowers, hidden, within itself,
and thanks to your love the tight aroma that arose
from the earth lives dimly in my body.

I love you without knowing how, or when, or from where,
I love you directly without problems or pride:
I love you like this because I don't know any other way to love,
except in this form in which I am not nor are you,
so close that your hand upon my chest is mine,
so close that your eyes close with my dreams.

PABLO NERUDA

Romantic

It's hard to mourn in shorts, a straw hat, flip-flops.
Cats from the sanctuary sunbathe nude
on the headstones, or cool the embassies
of themselves among the pomegranate trees.

Would the cicadas ever quit buckling their ribs.
A gecko goes bouldering over Antonio Gramsci's grave
and the beautiful teeth of American tourists are sparkling
but they can't help it, and we are tourists too.

We drink water by the jeroboam
and go over again the terrible things Percy Shelley did
in the name of his fireproof heart.
Die by drowning or don't – these remain our options.

The water cycle magics on like something
finer than a clock and John Keats
it's nice to meet you, under the circumstances.
And John Keats, please excuse us, time has made it late.

It's today already
and we have only the rest of our lives.
Long may we dabble our feet in the clear Italian lakes.
Long may we mosey through the graveyards of the world.

STEPHEN SEXTON

Sonnet XXX: 'Love is not all'

Love is not all: it is not meat nor drink
Nor slumber nor a roof against the rain;
Nor yet a floating spar to men that sink
And rise and sink and rise and sink again;
Love can not fill the thickened lung with breath,
Nor clean the blood, nor set the fractured bone;
Yet many a man is making friends with death
Even as I speak, for lack of love alone.
It well may be that in a difficult hour,
Pinned down by pain and moaning for release,
Or nagged by want past resolution's power,
I might be driven to sell your love for peace,
Or trade the memory of this night for food.
It well may be. I do not think I would.

EDNA ST VINCENT MILLAY

A Declaration of Need

I need you like a novel needs a plot.
I need you like the greedy needs a lot.
I need you like a hovel needs a certain level of grottiness
to qualify.
I need you like acne cream needs spottiness.
Like a calendar needs a week.
Like a colander needs a leek.
Like people need to seek out what life on Mars is.
Like hospitals need vases.
I need you.
I need you like a zoo needs a giraffe.
I need you like a psycho needs a path.
I need you like King Arthur needs a table
that was more than just a table for one.
I need you like a kiwi needs a fruit.
I need you like a wee wee needs a route out of the body.
I need you like Noddy needed little ears,
just for the contrast.
I need you like bone needs marrow.
I need you like straight needs narrow.
I need you like the broadest bean needs something else on the plate
before it can participate
in what you might describe as a decent meal.
I need you like a cappuccino needs froth.
I need you like a candle needs a moth
if it's going to burn its wings off.

JOHN HEGLEY

The Shape of Her

Somewhere a woman prepares to love another woman
for the first time and wonders: is she ready?

Going to love a woman is not like going to buy a dog.
She will not squeal and waggle her behind,

she will not pounce and jump on you. She will not pause
under the dwindling cherry blossom and catch the petals

to stick them on her nails, she will not sing *tirra lirra*
I don't know. Wait for the chill birdsong of evening.

She won't dwell in a Hotel Room, half-dressed,
reading Trollope in the daytime, like Edward Hopper, 1913.

She is not Cindy Sherman, lying on the floor with her dress
rolled up to her face: she is alive. There is no saying

what she'll say. Perhaps she does not want you. Here is
the shape of her. She is not a wardrobe, she is not

a box of toffee, she is not a pillow of cloud,
an old Baird wireless, nor a handsome Chesterfield. She is not

the Encyclopaedia Britannica; you will ask her things she cannot
answer; she will ask you what you're doing, you won't know.

You want to be her monkey, her mother, her lover, her beau,
her favourite aunt, little sister, toyboy, her big brother,

her box of Liquorice Allsorts, her dressing-up cupboard,
her joke polyurethane apron, Lady Penelope's pink

Rolls Royce, her gold cupid, her Sugar Puff engine,
her Swamp Thing, her fat grunting hog on a rope.

CHRISTINA DUNHILL

Love Poem

My love for you is like the Chesterfield canal, that first wall
with its spray-painted FUCK OFF, a gang of trees lining the bank
like hesitating divers, framed in the indifferent light, a single heron
and its tired, slow-motion flight towards the loading bay.
It's the Peugeot and the BMW exchanging stolen goods
an hour before dawn, parked where the path begins,
the secrecy of rain through the leaves at Brimington.
It's bee orchids and cuckoo spit, sunk, swollen mattresses,
a girl's reflection by the lock, the ghosts of narrow boats,
the lost dog who lives like a fox, split ear and puddled eyes,
roaming the undergrowth, finding the copse where a man
sleeps rough in his orange survival bag. It's the chairless
beer garden, the walkway that says DEATH TO UK COAL,
the ground they searched for the woman who never
came home. And my love for you is the light show
water makes beneath the Tapton bridge in summertime,
a shoal against the brickwork, shuddering, it's the crooked spire
and how it holds the sunset when you turn back towards town,
the watch you found in the long grass once,
still ticking, minute hand stuck over the hour

HELEN MORT

Pride's Crossing

Where the railroad meets the sea,
I recognise her hand.
Where the railroad meets the sea,
her hair is as intricate as a thumbprint.
Where the railroad meets the sea,
her name is the threshold of sleep.

Where the railroad meets the sea,
it takes all night to get there.
Where the railroad meets the sea,
you have stepped over the barrier.
Where the railroad meets the sea,
you will understand afterwards.

Where the railroad meets the sea,
where the railroad meets the sea –
I know only that our paths lie together,
and you cannot endure if you remain alone.

JAMES TATE

First Thought after Seeing You Smile

come with every wound
and every woman you've ever loved
every lie you've ever told
and whatever it is that keeps you up at night
every mouth you've ever punched in
all the blood you've ever tasted
come with every enemy you've ever made
and all the family you've ever buried
and every dirty thing you've ever done
every drink that's burnt your throat
and every morning you've woken
with nothing and no one
come with all your loss
your regrets, sins
memories
black outs
secrets
come with all the rot in your mouth
and that voice like needle hitting record
come with your kind eyes and weeping knuckles
come with all your shame
come with your swollen heart
i've never seen anything more beautiful than you.

WARSAN SHIRE

I Married You

I married you
for all the wrong reasons,
charmed by your
dangerous family history,
by the innocent muscles, bulging
like hidden weapons
under your shirt,
by your naive ties, the colors
of painted scraps of sunset.

I was charmed too
by your assumptions
about me: my serenity –
that mirror waiting to be cracked,
my flashy acrobatics with knives
in the kitchen.
How wrong we both were
about each other,
and how happy we have been.

LINDA PASTAN

Waiting

Left off the highway and
down the hill. At the
bottom, hang another left.
Keep bearing left. The road
will make a Y. Left again.
There's a creek on the left.
Keep going. Just before
the road ends, there'll be
another road. Take it
and no other. Otherwise,
your life will be ruined
forever. There's a log house
with a shake roof, on the left.
It's not that house. It's
the next house, just over
a rise. The house
where trees are laden with
fruit. Where phlox, forsythia,
and marigold grow. It's
the house where a woman
stands in the doorway
wearing the sun in her hair. The one
who's been waiting
all this time.
The woman who loves you.
The one who can say,
"What's kept you?"

RAYMOND CARVER

I Don't Want to Live a Small Life

I don't want to live a small life. Open your eyes,
open your hands. I have just come
from the berry fields, the sun

kissing me with its golden mouth all the way
(open your hands) and the wind-winged clouds
following along thinking perhaps I might

feed them, but no I carry these heart-shapes
only to you. Look how many small
but so sweet and maybe the last gift

I will bring to anyone in this
world of hope and risk, so do.
Look at me. Open your life, open your hands.

MARY OLIVER

Bridled Vows

I will be faithful to you, I do vow
but not until the seas have all run dry
et cetera: although I mean it now,
I'm not a prophet and I will not lie.
To be your perfect wife, I could not swear;
I'll love, yes; honour (maybe); won't obey,
but will co-operate if you will care
as much as you are seeming to today.
I'll do my best to be your better half,
but I don't have the patience of a saint;
not with you, at you I may sometimes laugh,
and snap too, though I'll try to learn restraint.
We might work out: no blame if we do not.
With all my heart, I think it's worth a shot.

IAN DUHIG

For the New House

May this house be full of kitchen smells
and shadows and toys and nests of mice
and roars of rage and waterfalls of tears
and deep sexual silences and sounds
of mysterious origin never explained
and troves and keepsakes and a lot of junk
and a flowing like a warm wind only slower
blowing the leaves of trees and books and the fish-years
of a child's life silvery flickering
quick, quick, in the slow incessant gust
that billows out the curtains for a moment
all those years from now, ago.
May the sills and doorframes
be in blessing blest at every passing.
May the roof but not the rooms know rain.
May the windows know clearly
the branch and flower of the apple tree.
And may you be in this house
as the music is in the instrument.

URSULA K. LE GUIN

I Wanna Be Yours

let me be your vacuum cleaner
breathing in your dust
let me be your ford cortina
i will never rust
if you like your coffee hot
let me be your coffee pot
you call the shots
i wanna be yours

let me be your raincoat
for those frequent rainy days
let me be your dreamboat
when you wanna sail away
let me be your teddy bear
take me with you anywhere
i don't care
i wanna be yours

let me be your electric meter
i will not run out
let me be the electric heater
you get cold without
let me be your setting lotion
hold your hair with deep devotion
deep as the deep Atlantic ocean
that's how deep is my emotion
deep deep deep deep de deep deep
i don't wanna be hers
i wanna be yours

JOHN COOPER CLARKE

Poem

Loving you is every bit as fine
as coming over a hill into the sun
at ninety miles an hour darling when
it's dawn and you can hear the stars unlocking
themselves from the designs of God beneath
the disintegrating orchestra of my black
Chevrolet. The radio clings to an un-
identified station somewhere a tango suffers,
and the dance floor burns around two lovers
whom nothing can touch – no, not even death!
Oh! the acceleration with which my heart does proceed,
reaching like stars almost but never quite
of light the speed of light the speed of light.

DENIS JOHNSON

Marriage Song

God said (and already you can tell
I'm making this up),

Let this woman and this man
Be joined together

In front of the sea and the grass
And the trees who don't care

He said, Let them make
A gate in themselves

Through which the other can pass
And may the gate never be closed

So they can feel the truth of being entered

And the loneliness of being
Imperfectly misunderstood –

Now go, God said,
Into the country of love

Change it with your experiments
Don't be intimidated Enjoy your skin

Impress me
Make something grow

For your bravery merely in undertaking
This impossible task

I make you a special loan called Time
No, don't bother to thank me now –

You can pay me back as you go

TONY HOAGLAND

For Keeps

Sun makes the day new.
Tiny green plants emerge from earth.
Birds are singing the sky into place.
There is nowhere else I want to be but here.
I lean into the rhythm of your heart to see where it will take us.
We gallop into a warm, southern wind.
I link my legs to yours and we ride together,
Toward the ancient encampment of our relatives.
Where have you been? they ask.
And what has taken you so long?
That night after eating, singing, and dancing
We lay together under the stars.
We know ourselves to be part of mystery.
It is unspeakable.
It is everlasting.
It is for keeps.

JOY HARJO

Romantic Comedy

I had been worrying somewhat
about the final scene –
where to set it
and what could be the hero's
extravagant gesture?

But then I realised
how these things end.
He just shows up.
He just shows up
and says *I love you.*

LORRAINE MARINER

O Small Sad Ecstasy of Love

I like being with you all night with closed eyes.
What luck – here you are
coming
along the stars!
I did a road trip
all over my mind and heart
and
there you were
kneeling by the roadside
with your little toolkit
fixing something.

Give me a world, you have taken the world I was.

ANNE CARSON

When I hear your name

When I hear your name
I feel a little robbed of it;
it seems unbelievable
that half a dozen letters could say so much.

My compulsion is to blast down every wall with your name
I'd paint it on all the houses
there wouldn't be a well
I hadn't leaned into
to shout your name there,
nor a stone mountain
where I hadn't uttered
those six separate letters
that are echoed back.

My compulsion is
to teach the birds to sing it,
to teach the fish to drink it,
to teach men that there is nothing
like the madness of repeating your name.

My compulsion is to forget altogether
the other 22 letters, all the numbers,
the books I've read, the poems I've written.
To say hello with your name.
To beg bread with your name.
'She always says the same thing,' they'd say when they saw me,
and I'd be so proud, so happy, so self-contained.

And I'll go to the other world with your name on my tongue,
and all their questions I'll answer with your name

– the judges and saints will understand nothing –
God will sentence me to repeating it endlessly and forever.

GLORIA FUERTES

Science

I was delighted when my scientist girlfriend agreed to become my fiancée. 'This is the happiest moment of my life', I said.

'Mine, too', she replied. 'I'm experiencing an unprecedented rush of dopamine and norepinephrine. Of course the production of these particular neurotransmitters will decrease over time, but I have a pretty good feeling that our vasopressin levels will remain adequate, and we'll be fine for the long haul. But never mind all that', she said, taking off her goggles and unbuttoning her lab coat. 'What do you say we release a bit of the old oxytocin?'

DAN RHODES

7301

Learning to read you, twenty years ago,
Over the pub lunch cheese-and-onion rolls.

Learning you eat raw onions; learning your taste
For obscurity, how you encode teachers & classrooms

As the hands, the shop floor; learning to hide
The sudden shining naked looks of love. And thinking

The rest of our lives, the rest of our lives
Doing perfectly ordinary things together – riding

In buses, walking in Sainsbury's, sitting
In pubs eating cheese-and-onion rolls,

All those tomorrows. Now twenty years after,
We've had seventy-three hundred of them, and

(If your arithmetic's right, & our luck) we may
Fairly reckon on seventy-three hundred more.

I hold them crammed in my arms, colossal crops
Of shining tomorrows that may never happen,

But may they! Still learning to read you,
To hear what it is you're saying, to master the code.

U. A. FANTHORPE

Honeymooners' Ghazal

You teach me the name of each bird, my love,
and I test on my tongue every word, my love.

A redshank now boomerangs in towards shore,
where her water-flute cry can be heard, my love.

At Mull Head's rocky ledge, dark cormorants stand
and survey the white spume churned to curd, my love.

A gannet's beak pierces the linen of mist,
pulling fast an invisible cord, my love.

When a sea-fret blows in from the coast then exhales,
once again you're beside me, unblurred, my love.

A crow in a hood flaps its course into squall
round the cliffs of Deerness, undeterred, my love.

These kittiwakes glide – they trace rings with their wings
and your voice is the air that they've stirred, my love.

KATHRYN BEVIS

'It was as if I were asleep'

It was as if I were asleep the whole of my life and I didn't know a thing, nothing on the inside, not that life was life, or death is death, how I was right or how I was wrong, that nothing lasts and there's no one to blame, and nobody gets out of it, not even you, not even me, nobody gets out of it alive, but as long as I live, come to me, as long as my love has the strength of the blood that gives life and the grief of the blood that drains away, come to me wired and wild like the bare tree and the shedding sky . . .

after Mary Oliver
& Tina Turner

EMILY BERRY

Transformation

I haven't written a single poem
in months.
I've lived humbly, reading the paper,
pondering the riddle of power
and the reasons for obedience.
I've watched sunsets
(crimson, anxious),
I've heard the birds grow quiet
and night's muteness.
I've seen sunflowers dangling
their heads at dusk, as if a careless hangman
had gone strolling through the gardens.
September's sweet dust gathered
on the windowsill and lizards
hid in the bends of walls.
I've taken long walks,
craving one thing only:
lightning,
transformation,
you.

ADAM ZAGAJEWSKI, TRANSLATED BY
CLARE CAVANAGH

When You Are Near, I Turn into a Baja Fairy Duster

By which I mean I look like that flower that fireworks in
   mid-sentence
in the sky, over the end of a sweaty ball game. The crowd
   makes its way
to their cars while popcorn-spill & multicolored chocolate
   candies melt
into concrete steps. Maybe I mean you make me want to live
beachfront – so I can taste the salt & cliff-twist on each red
   stamen.
When you're near, you call hummingbirds to my throat & we
   throw
our heads back and stomp our feet from laughing too loud in
   a café.
I make good tears in my eyes which means joy & maybe
   emerald feathers
fall to the floor. All the other patrons turn to glare: how dare
   we delight
in the swoop of blossom & neck. I know it sounds like turning
into a plant would not be fun, but have you seen a baja fairy
   duster? The way
it shocks the mountain trail, how it asterisks all year round?
   Perhaps you think
I'd be sad to rely on sunlight & sea spray, that I would wither
   in the dark,
but trust me – some people wait whole pink & proper lives to
   feel this even once.

AIMEE NEZHUKUMATATHIL

The Year We Married Birds

That year, with men turning thirty
still refusing to fly the nest,
we married birds instead.

Migrating snow buntings
swept into offices in the city,
took flocks of girls for Highland weddings.

Magpies smashed jewellers' windows,
kites hovered above bridal shops,
a pigeon in Trafalgar Square learnt to kneel.

Sales of nesting boxes soared.
Soon cinemas were wild as woods in May
while restaurants served worms.

By June, a Russian kittiwake wed
the Minister's daughter, gave her two
freckled eggs, a mansion on a cliff.

My own groom was a kingfisher:
enigmatic, bright. He gleamed in a metallic
turquoise suit, taught me about fishing

in the murky canal. We honeymooned
near the Wash, the saltmarshes
booming with courting bittern.

When I think of that year, I remember best
the fanning of his feathers
on my cheek, his white throat,

how every building, every street rang
with birdsong. How girls' wedding dresses
lifted them into the trees like wings.

LIZ BERRY

Wedding Weather

September: the last, dry neon-headed match
left in the box soaked by long weeks of rain
makes good. A day – then two, then three days, catch . . .
the sky is blue as a bunsen-burner flame
and with the whiff of sea-salt, the high cries
at evening time, and late, unlikely sales
in plastic spades and buckets, come the days
long marked in diaries, cleared on schedules –
a season of surprise festivities.

The boys have had their final 'final drink'.
The girls who said *they'd never marry* are
– some of them to other girls. To think
of the effort put in just to get this far:
the venue chosen; lists; who to invite;
the card found with its quirky print – a style
agreed by both (*no hearts, no church, no white*);
the comic tune for walking down the aisle
(Darth Vader's theme?) worked so it's *them*, and *right*.

I think this is the day four thousand dawns
that faltered at the door and did not break
– or broke, in procession, on low, wintry rooms
where we slept on, at home, or where we'd wake
and be lone and whole (and missing something, true,
but not *one simple thing* we recognised
in someone else) – might yet have led us to:
at last our inner sad selves synthesised
with those figures up there, smiling, in full view.

LEONTIA FLYNN

blessing the boats

(at St. Mary's)

may the tide
that is entering even now
the lip of our understanding
carry you out
beyond the face of fear
may you kiss
the wind then turn from it
certain that it will
love your back   may you
open your eyes to water
water waving forever
and may you in your innocence
sail through this to that

LUCILLE CLIFTON

from Twenty-One Love Poems

II

I wake up in your bed. I know I have been dreaming.
Much earlier, the alarm broke us from each other,
you've been at your desk for hours. I know what I dreamed:
our friend the poet comes into my room
where I've been writing for days,
drafts, carbons, poems are scattered everywhere,
and I want to show her one poem
which is the poem of my life. But I hesitate,
and wake. You've kissed my hair
to wake me. *I dreamed you were a poem,*
I say, *a poem I wanted to show someone* . . .
and I laugh and fall dreaming again
of the desire to show you to everyone I love,
to move openly together
in the pull of gravity, which is not simple,
which carries the feathered grass a long way down the
    upbreathing air.

ADRIENNE RICH

Saying Something

Things assume your shape; discarded clothes, a damp shroud
in the bathroom, vacant hands. This is not fiction. This is
the plain and warm material of love. My heart assumes it.

We wake. Our private language starts the day. We make
familiar movements through the house. The dreams we have
no phrases for slip through our fingers into smoke.

I dreamed I was not with you. Wandering in a city
where you did not live, I stared at strangers, searching
for a word to make them you. I woke beside you.

Sweetheart, I say. Pedestrian daylight terms scratch
darker surfaces. Your absence leaves me with the ghost
of love; half-warm coffee cups or sheets, the gentlest kiss.

Walking home, I see you turning on the lights. I come in
from outside calling your name, saying something.

CAROL ANN DUFFY

The Present

For the present there is just one moon,
though every level pond gives back another.

But the bright disc shining in the black lagoon,
perceived by astrophysicist and lover,

is milliseconds old. And even that light's
seven minutes older than its source.

And the stars we think we see on moonless nights
are long extinguished. And, of course,

this very moment, as you read this line,
is literally gone before you know it.

Forget the here-and-now. We have no time
but this device of wantonness and wit.

Make me this present then: your hand in mine,
and we'll live out our lives in it.

MICHAEL DONAGHY

in your kitchen

one of us kneeling at the oven door
we're baking our own wedding cake
your hands on the wet cutlery   ginger
shedding into a mixing bowl I trust
my gut   your dancer's fingers always
quick stepping at my pelvis   half moon
– walking down my apron   touch
starved like we are practicing worship
functional love godly
domesticity

I tell you where it's not hurting   but it is
tender & which parts of me are overdue
for a firmer elbow   your upper lip
smudged from all the oil we've been
cooking with   we barely weigh
a thing   in our hats

with wide brims   you can't kiss
my face   we can't look up   beloved
there's no need
there isn't anything higher.

KATIE O'PRAY

I promise when I lift your egg

from the water with my special spoon,
carry it to a cup as if it were a bald man
whistling steam to a tune he had just made up;
when I take my green handled egg-knife
to whip off the top and inside it is more
than yellow, like a laugh about to happen,
or butter pushed into light; when you dunk
gorgeously in, softly exploding the yolk
like a new idea finding one coloured term
for its articulation; when the little promise
of the egg, contained inside from the moment
it was laid, is broken by your tongue, then,
like love, it is remade, I promise.

JACK UNDERWOOD

This One's for You

I edited the first love poem he wrote me
before he'd even sent it. He'd only
told me about it, said that he was
penning something.
I winced. Corrected all the punctuation
and grammar. He doesn't like commas much.
I sieved it for clichés and abstractions.
Converted the ethereal to concrete.
All the sky into grit.
When it was finished, as finished
as it was ever going to be, and a lot
shorter than anticipated, I said,
here, baby, here it is. This one's for you.

RACHEL LONG

Pull Out All the Stops

Dear –
I love you so much   I had to
write it somewhere   so
I am writing it
on the back of a receipt for apple strudel
in the British Museum café.
(There.
That feels better already.)
Can you imagine
what you'd do to me in bed?
You could make me pay for
all the slights   the irritating
enigmas   the deliberate
inattention.   I hope so.
Make me pay   and pay again.
Like Dante
in that stony rhyming of his
desire to pin Beatrice down
twisting his fingers into her rope of hair
as she cries out through
all the hours   rung by
monks' bells   all through the long
medieval Tuscan day.
(Except
he never did.)
You can't think   I'm up to constructing
another heaven?
I can't think   either.

This process of revision
final and   first touches!
I wrote this with my own hand:
never let me go again   my love.

ANTHONY VAHNI CAPILDEO

'Let me put it this way'

Let me put it this way:
if you came to lay

your sleeping head
against my arm or sleeve,

and if my arm went dead,
or if I had to take my leave

at midnight, I should rather
cleave it from the joint or seam

than make a scene
or bring you round.

There,
how does that sound?

SIMON ARMITAGE

One Enchanted Evening

You found me in quicksand
and did not ask me stupid questions.
You peeled a mandarin drake
and did not ask me to watch.
You sent away the doctors
and the doctors of the church.
You photographed an indigo mosquito hawk
and showed me the result.
You crosshatched something in a book
and lowered the brim of your hat.
You touched a long pole to the top of my head
and walked in circles around me.
You kept the measure of the distance between us
inside a secret pocket.
You pried open an oyster
and kept your eyes shut.
You poured yourself a glass of cold vodka
and did not offer me any.
You picked up a dispatch in a bottle
and did not ask me to witness it.
You brought me a lop-eared rabbit
and let me watch it sleep.
You showed me a cicada still in its tuxedo
and let me watch it eat an elder leaf.
Seasons came and seasons went
and in between a boy and girl grew up.
You did not ask me what that was about.
You sang awhile to the stars and the wind
and did not let me stop you.

DARA WIER

Honeymoon at Weybourne

The cog rattle of the sea sucking
pebbles was so immense we almost

didn't get in. We floated on a strong
tide which pulled us up the coast, away

from our things. After you'd had
your fill and left me to loll in the waves

I watched you watch me from the ridge,
blue in my towel against the burnt orange cliffs

and though the tide still pulled I didn't drift.
I kept my eyes on you: marker, anchor, wife.

LUKE WRIGHT

Wife

Strange to use this word
for the woman I love –

is she my wife
when she lays her head on my shoulder,

when I whisper her name
in the morning to see if she's awake,

or when we plant bluebells
under the oak

where we buried one dog, three cats
and a handful of dreams?

I practice saying *Isobel is my wife*
and it sings to the tune of my life.

JANE CLARKE

The Amnesty

I surrender my weapons:
Catapult Tears, Raincloud Hat,
Lip Zip, Brittle Coat, Taut Teeth
in guarded rows. Pluck this plate
of armour from my ear, drop
it in the Amnesty Bin,
watch my sadness land among
the dark shapes of memory.

Unarmed, now see me saunter
past Ticking Baggage, Loaded
Questions, Gangs of Doubt; my love
equips me. I swear, ever
since your cheeky face span round
I trust this whole bloody world.

CAROLINE BIRD

True Love

True love. Is it normal,
is it serious, is it practical?
What does the world get from two people
who exist in a world of their own?

Placed on the same pedestal for no good reason,
drawn randomly from millions but convinced
it had to happen this way – in reward for what? For nothing.
The light descends from nowhere.
Why on these two and not on others?
Doesn't this outrage justice? Yes it does.
Doesn't it disrupt our painstakingly erected principles,
and cast the moral from the peak? Yes on both accounts.

Look at the happy couple.
Couldn't they at least try to hide it,
fake a little depression for their friends' sake!
Listen to them laughing – it's an insult.
The language they use – deceptively clear.
And their little celebrations, rituals,
the elaborate mutual routines –
it's obviously a plot behind the human race's back!

It's hard even to guess how far things might go
if people start to follow their example.
What could religion and poetry count on?
What would be remembered? What renounced?
Who'd want to stay within bounds?

True love. Is it really necessary?
Tact and common sense tell us to pass over it in silence,
like a scandal in Life's highest circles.
Perfectly good children are born without its help.
It couldn't populate the planet in a million years,
it comes along so rarely.

Let the people who never find true love
keep saying that there's no such thing.

Their faith will make it easier for them to live and die.

WISŁAWA SZYMBORSKA

I Remember

By the first of August
the invisible beetles began
to snore and the grass was
as tough as hemp and was
no colour – no more than
the sand was a color and
we had worn our bare feet
bare since the twentieth
of June and there were times
we forgot to wind up your
alarm clock and some nights
we took our gin warm and neat
from old jelly glasses while
the sun blew out of sight
like a red picture hat and
one day I tied my hair back
with a ribbon and you said
that I look almost like
a puritan lady and what
I remember best is that
the door to your room was
the door to mine.

ANNE SEXTON

Two Lighthouses

I would like us to live like two lighthouses
at the mouth of a river, each with her own lamp.

We could see each other across the water,
which would be dangerous, and uncrossable.

I could watch your shape, your warm shadow,
moving in the upper rooms. We would have jokes.

Jokes that were only ours, signs and secrets,
flares on birthdays, a rocket at Christmas.

Clouds would be cities, we would look for omens,
and learn the impossible language of birds.

We would meet, of course, in cinemas, cafés,
but then, we would return to our towers,

knowing the other was the light on the water,
a beam of alignment. It would never be broken.

JULIA DARLING

Prayer for a Marriage

When we are old one night and the moon
arcs over the house like an antique
china saucer and the teacup sun

follows somewhere far behind
I hope the stars deepen to a shine
so bright you could read by it

if you liked and the sadness
we will have known go away
for a while – in this hour or two

before sleep – and that we kiss
standing in the kitchen not fighting
gravity so much as embodying

its sweet force, and I hope we kiss
like we do today knowing so much
good is said in this primitive tongue

from the wild first surprising ones
to the lower dizzy ten thousand
infinitely slower ones – and I hope

while we stand there in the kitchen
making tea and kissing, the whistle
of the teapot wakes the neighbours.

STEVE SCAFIDI

Sonnets from the Portuguese XIV: 'If thou must love me'

If thou must love me, let it be for nought
Except for love's sake only. Do not say
'I love her for her smile – her look – her way
Of speaking gently, – for a trick of thought
That falls in well with mine, and certes brought
A sense of pleasant ease on such a day' –
For these things in themselves, Belovèd, may
Be changed, or change for thee, – and love, so wrought,
May be unwrought so. Neither love me for
Thine own dear pity's wiping my cheeks dry, –
A creature might forget to weep, who bore
Thy comfort long, and lose thy love thereby!
But love me for love's sake, that evermore
Thou may'st love on, through love's eternity.

ELIZABETH BARRETT BROWNING

Mountain Dew Commercial Disguised as a Love Poem

So here's what I've got, the reasons why our marriage
might work: Because you wear pink but write poems
about bullets and gravestones. Because you yell
at your keys when you lose them, and laugh,
loudly, at your own jokes. Because you can hold a pistol,
gut a pig. Because you memorize songs, even commercials
from thirty years back and sing them when vacuuming.
You have soft hands. Because when we moved, the contents
of what you packed were written inside the boxes.
Because you think swans are overrated and kind of stupid.
Because you drove me to the train station. You drove me
to Minneapolis. You drove me to Providence.
Because you underline everything you read, and circle
the things you think are important, and put stars next
to the things you think I should think are important,
and write notes in the margins about all the people
you're mad at and my name almost never appears there.
Because you made that pork recipe you found
in the Frida Kahlo Cookbook. Because when you read
that essay about Rilke, you underlined the whole thing
except the part where Rilke says love means to deny the self
and to be consumed in flames. Because when the lights
are off, the curtains drawn, and an additional sheet is nailed
over the windows, you still believe someone outside
can see you. And one day five summers ago,
when you couldn't put gas in your car, when your fridge
was so empty – not even leftovers or condiments –
there was a single twenty-ounce bottle of Mountain Dew,

which you paid for with your last damn dime
because you once overheard me say that I liked it.

MATTHEW OLZMANN

The Dereliction

Love me like that pub on Darkhouse Lane,
sweetheart of wet-the-beds and creeping rot.

Love me like I have no windows, no doors, just wild
blue streaming through unarrested.

Love me to the bare bones, through rain and rough weather,
time singing its song of *dereliction dereliction*.

Touch your palms to my walls, their yielding brick,
and remember how my face held its look

of abandon, how young we were, my white dress lifted
and blown reckless as a kite in a storm.

LIZ BERRY

I Loved You Before I Was Born

I loved you before I was born.
It doesn't make sense, I know.

I saw your eyes before I had eyes to see.
And I've lived longing
for your every look ever since.
That longing entered time as this body.
And the longing grew as this body waxed.
And the longing grows as the body wanes.
The longing will outlive this body.

I loved you before I was born.
It makes no sense, I know.

Long before eternity, I caught a glimpse
of your neck and shoulders, your ankles and toes.
And I've been lonely for you from that instant.
That loneliness appeared on earth as this body.
And my share of time has been nothing
but your name outrunning my ever saying it clearly.
Your face fleeing my ever
kissing it firmly once on the mouth.

In longing, I am most myself, rapt,
my lamp mortal, my light
hidden and singing.

I give you my blank heart.
Please write on it
what you wish.

LI-YOUNG LEE

Acknowledgements

We would like to thank each and every poet who makes up this anthology of alternative wedding poems. Thank you for making us believe a little more in love while we sat last summer in the Poetry Library poring over piles and piles of books. Thank you to the Poetry Library for so kindly offering us the space to work. Thank you especially to Troy Cabida who ever-graciously helped us pull out collection after collection. No request was too much bother.

A special thank you to Emma Paterson. To Aparna Kumar. And, of course, to the Picador team; to Colette Bryce for believing in the idea from the bat, to Ebruba Abel-Unokan, Nicholas Blake, and Mary Mount, for all your work realising this project.

Copyright Acknowledgements

The publishers are grateful to the following for permission to reproduce copyright material.

Kim Addonizio, 'Like That', from *Tell Me*. Copyright © 2000 by Kim Addonizio. Reprinted with the permission of The Permissions Company, LLC on behalf of BOA Editions, Ltd., boaeditions.org.

Maya Angelou, 'Come. And Be My Baby', from *Oh Pray My Wings Are Gonna Fit Me Well* by Maya Angelou. Copyright © 1975 by Caged Bird Legacy, LLC. Used by permission of Random House, an imprint and division of Penguin Random House LLC. All rights reserved.

Simon Armitage, 'Let me put it this way', from *Book of Matches* (Faber and Faber Limited).

Margaret Atwood, 'Habitation', from *Selected Poems I: 1965–1975* (Mariner, 1987). Reprinted by kind permission of Curtis Brown Limited.

Margaret Atwood, 'Variations on the Word Love', from *True Stories* (Oxford University Press, 1981).

Emily Berry, 'It was as if I were asleep', from *Unexhausted Time* (Faber and Faber Limited).

Liz Berry, 'The Dereliction', from *The Dereliction* (Hercules Editions, 2021).

Liz Berry, 'The Year We Married Birds', from *Black Country* (Chatto & Windus). Copyright © Liz Berry, 2014. Reprinted by permission of The Random House Group Limited.

Kathryn Bevis, 'Honeymooner's Ghazal', from *The Butterfly House* (Seren Books, 2024).

Caroline Bird, 'Meghan Married Herself', from *In These Days of Prohibition* (Carcanet Press, 2017).

Caroline Bird, 'The Amnesty', from *In These Days of Prohibition* (Carcanet Press, 2017).

Hera Lindsay Bird, 'I want to get high my whole life with you', from *Pamper Me to Hell & Back* (Smith|Doorstop, 2018).

Lewis Buxton, 'A Boy Gets Married', from *Boy in Various Poses* (Nine Arches Press, 2021). Published by permission of Nine Arches Press. www.ninearchespress.com

Anthony Vahni Capildeo, 'Pull Out All the Stops', *Utter* (Peepal Tree Press, 2013).

Anne Carson, 'O Small Sad Ecstasy of Love'. Originally published in Poem-a-Day on December 10, 2020, by the Academy of American Poets. Copyright © Anne Carson 2020. Reprinted by permission of Aragi Inc.

Anne Carson, 'Short Talk on the Sensation of Aeroplane Takeoff', from *Short Talks* (Brick Books, 1992). Reprinted by permission of Aragi Inc.

Raymond Carver, 'Waiting', from *All of Us: The Collected Poems* by Raymond Carver. Copyright © 1996 by Raymond Carver. Used by permission of Random House, an imprint and division of Penguin Random House LLC. All rights reserved.

Chen Chen, 'I love you to the moon &.', originally published in Poem-a-Day on May 31, 2021, by the Academy of American Poets. Copyright © Chen Chen 2021. Reprinted by kind permission of the author.

Jane Clarke, 'Wife', from *A Change in the Air* (Bloodaxe Books, 2023).

Lucille Clifton, 'blessing the boats', from *Blessing the Boats* by Lucille Clifton, published by Penguin Classics. Copyright © Lucille Clifton, 2001. Reprinted by permission of The Random House Group Limited.

Andrea Cohen, 'Contingency'. Reprinted by kind permission of Andrea Cohen.

John Cooper Clarke, 'I Wanna Be Yours', from *Ten Years in an Open Necked Shirt* by John Cooper Clarke (Vintage). Copyright © April Music, 1977. Reprinted by permission of The Random House Group Limited.

Julia Darling, 'Two Lighthouses', from *Apology for Absence* (Arc Publications, 2005). © Estate of Julia Darling.

Michael Donaghy, 'The Present', from *Collected Poems* (Picador, 2014). Copyright © Michael Donaghy 1988.

Carol Ann Duffy, 'Saying Something', from *Standing Female Nude* (Picador, 2016). Copyright © Carol Ann Duffy 1985.

Carol Ann Duffy, 'White Writing', from *Feminine Gospels* (Picador, 2002). Copyright © Carol Ann Duffy 2002.

Ian Duhig, 'Bridled Vows', from *New and Selected Poems* (Picador, 2021). Copyright © Ian Duhig 2021.

Ian Duhig, 'From The Irish', from *The Bradford Count* (Bloodaxe Books, 1991).

Christina Dunhill, 'The Shape of Her', from *Anvil New Poets 2* (Anvil Press Poetry, 1995).

Stephen Dunn, 'The Kiss'. Copyright © 2008 by Stephen Dunn, from *Everything Else in the World* by Stephen Dunn. Used by permission of W.W. Norton & Company, Inc.

Leontia Flynn, 'Wedding Weather', from *Profit and Loss* by Leontia Flynn (Jonathan Cape). Copyright © 2011, Leontia Flynn. Reprinted by permission of The Random House Group Limited.

Gloria Fuertes, 'When I hear your name', from *Off the Map* (Wesleyan University Press, 1984).

Linda Gregg, 'The Weight', from *All of It Singing: New and Selected Poems*. Copyright © 1994 by Linda Gregg. Reprinted with the permission of The Permissions Company, LLC on behalf of Graywolf Press, www.graywolfpress.org.

Jen Hadfield, 'Nigh-No-Place', from *Nigh-No-Place* (Bloodaxe Books, 2008).

Donald Hall, 'Gold', from *Old and New Poems* (Ticknor and Fields, 1990). Reprinted by permission of HarperCollins.

Joy Harjo, 'For Keeps'. Copyright © 2015 by Joy Harjo, from *Conflict Resolution for Holy Beings* by Joy Harjo. Used by permission of W.W. Norton & Company, Inc.

Jake Hawkey, 'Friday Night Drift', from *But & Though* (Picador, 2025). Copyright © Jake Hawkey 2025.

Seamus Heaney, 'Scaffolding', from *Death of a Naturalist* by Seamus Heaney (Faber and Faber Limited).

John Hegley, 'A Declaration of Need', from *New and Selected Potatoes* (Bloodaxe Books, 2013).

Essex Hemphill, 'American Wedding', from *Love is a Dangerous Word: the Selected Poems of Essex Hemphill* (New Directions, 2025). Reprinted by kind permission of New Directions.

Selima Hill, 'For Days Now I Have Been Imagining It', from *Gloria: Selected Poems* (Bloodaxe Books, 2008).

Selima Hill, 'The Wedding Dress', from *Women in Comfortable Shoes* (Bloodaxe Books, 2023).

Jane Hirshfield, 'For What Binds Us', from *Of Gravity and Angels* (Wesleyan University Press, 1988).

Tony Hoagland, 'Marriage Song', from *Priest Turned Therapist Treats Fear of God*. Copyright © 2018 by Tony Hoagland. Reprinted with the permission of The Permissions Company, LLC on behalf of Graywolf Press, www.graywolfpress.org.

Kathleen Jamie, 'The Stags', from *The Overhaul* (Picador, 2012). Copyright © Kathleen Jamie 2012.

Denis Johnson, 'Poem', from *The Veil* by Denis Johnson. Copyright © 1987 by Denis Johnson. Used by permission of Random House, an imprint and division of Penguin Random House LLC. All rights reserved.

Jackie Kay, 'A Lang Promise', from *Bantam* (Picador, 2017). Copyright © Jackie Kay 2017.

Nick Laird, 'Epithalamium', from *Go Giants* (Faber and Faber Limited).

Ursula K Le Guin, 'For the New House', from *Wild Oats & Fireweed* (Harper & Row, 1988). Reprinted by kind permission of Ginger Clark Literary.

Edward Lear, 'The Owl and the Pussy-Cat', from *Nonsense Songs, Stories, Botany, and Alphabets* (Robert John Bush, London, 1871).

Li-Young Lee, 'I Loved You Before I Was Born', from *The Undressing*. Copyright © 2018 by Li-Young Lee. Used by permission of W.W. Norton & Company, Inc.

Ada Limon, 'What I Didn't Know Before' and 'Love Poem with Apologies for My Appearance', from *The Carrying*. Copyright © 2018 by Ada Limón. Reprinted with the permission of The Permissions Company LLC on behalf of Milkweed Editions, milkweed.org.

Timothy Liu, 'The Lovers', from *Don't Go Back to Sleep* (Saturnalia Books, 2014).

Theresa Lola, 'Measuring Light', from *Ceremony for the Nameless* (Penguin Books). Copyright © Theresa Lola, 2024. Reprinted by permission of The Random House Group Limited.

Lorraine Mariner, 'Romantic Comedy', from *There Will Be No More Nonsense* (Picador, 2014). Copyright © Lorraine Mariner 2014.

Kei Miller, 'A Prayer at Squire Street 2009', from *A Light Song of Light* (Carcanet Press, 2010). Reprinted by permission of David Higham Associates.

Dorothy Molloy, 'Eternity Ring', from *Hare Soup* (Faber and Faber Limited).

Dorothy Molloy, 'Small Wedding', from *Hare Soup* (Faber and Faber Limited).

Kim Moore, 'In Another Life', from *The Art of Falling* (Seren Books, 2015).

Helen Mort, 'Love Poem', from *The Illustrated Woman* by Helen Mort (Chatto & Windus). Copyright © Helen Mort, 2022. Reprinted by permission of The Random House Group Limited.

Maggie Nelson, 'Promise', from *Something Bright, Then Holes*. Copyright © 2018 by Maggie Nelson. Reprinted with the permission of The Permissions Company LLC, on behalf of Soft Skull Press, an imprint of Counterpoint Press, softskull.com

Pablo Neruda, 'One Hundred Love Sonnets: XVII', from *The Essential Neruda: Selected Poems* (Bloodaxe Books, 2010).

Aimee Nezhukumatathil, 'When You Are Near, I Turn into a Baja Fairyduster', *Ploughshares*, Volume 45, Number 1 (2019). Reprinted by permission of the author.

Golnoosh Nour, 'Cat Worship', from *Rocksong*, VERVE Poetry Press, 2021. Reprinted by permission of Verve Poetry Press.

Naomi Shihab Nye, 'San Antonio', from *Is This Forever, Or What? Poems and Paintings from Texas*, Greenwillow, 2004. Reprinted by permission of HarperCollins.

Frank O'Hara, 'Having a Coke with You', from *The Collected Poems of Frank O'Hara*. Copyright © 1971 by Maureen Granville-Smith, Administratrix of the Estate of Frank O'Hara. Used by permission of Alfred A. Knopf, an imprint of the Knopf Doubleday Publishing Group, a division of Penguin Random House LLC. All rights reserved.

Katie O'Pray, 'In your kitchen', from *apricot* (Out-Spoken Press, 2022).

Sharon Olds, 'The Wedding Vow', from *The Unswept Room*. Copyright © 2002 by Sharon Olds. Used by permission of Alfred A. Knopf, an imprint of the Knopf Doubleday Publishing Group, a division of Penguin Random House LLC. All rights reserved.

Mary Oliver, 'I don't want to live a small life'. Reprinted by the permission of The Charlotte Sheedy Literary Agency as agent for the author. Copyright © 2008 by Mary Oliver with permission of Bill Reichblum.

Matthew Olzmann, 'Mountain Dew Commercial Disguised as a Love Poem', from *Mezzanines*. Copyright © 2013 by Matthew Olzmann. Reprinted with the permission of The Permissions Company, LLC on behalf of Alice James Books, alicejamesbooks.org.

Linda Pastan, 'I Married You', from *Queen of a Rainy Country*. Copyright © 2006 by Linda Pastan. Used by permission of W.W. Norton & Company, Inc.

Michael Pederson, 'Obsessive Cannibal Love Poem', from *Oyster* (Polygon, 2017).

Willie Perdomo, 'That's My Heart Right There', from *The Crazy Bunch* by Willie Perdomo. Copyright © 2019 by Willie Perdomo. Used by permission of Penguin Books, an imprint and division of Penguin Random House LLC. All rights reserved.

Natasha Rao, 'Cornucopia', *The Atlantic* (2024). Reprinted by permission of the author.

Dan Rhodes, 'Science', from *Marry Me* (Canongate Books, 2013).

Adrienne Rich, 'Twenty-One Love Poems: II', from *The Dream of a Common Language: Poems 1974–1977*. Copyright © 1978 by W.W. Norton & Company, Inc. Used by permission of W.W. Norton & Company, Inc.

Muriel Rukeyser, 'Looking at Each Other', from *Breaking Open*. Copyright © 1973 by Muriel Rukeyser. Used by permission of Random House, an imprint and division of Penguin Random House LLC. All rights reserved.

Sappho, ['It's no use / Mother dear . . .], from *Sappho: A New Translation*, trans. Mary Barnard, (University of California Press, 1958).

Steve Scafidi, 'Prayer for a Marriage', from *Sparks from a Nine-Pound Hammer* (Louisiana State University Press, 2001).

Anne Sexton, 'I Remember', from *All My Pretty Ones* (Houghton Mifflin Harcourt, 1962). Reprinted by kind permission of Sterling Lord Literistic and the Estate of Anne Sexton.

Anne Sexton, 'The Kiss', from *Love Poems* (Mariner Books, 1969). Reprinted by permission of HarperCollins.

Stephen Sexton, 'Romantic', from *Cheryl's Destinies* (Penguin). Copyright © 2021 Stephen Sexton. Reprinted by permission of The Random House Group Limited.

Clare Shaw, 'Vow', from *Head On* (Bloodaxe Books, 2012).

Warsan Shire, 'First Thought After Seeing You Smile', from *Bless The Daughter Raised by a Voice in Her Head* (Chatto & Windus). Copyright © Warsan Shire 2022.

Wislawa Szymborska, 'True Love', from *Map: Collected and Last Poems*, trans. Clare Cavanagh and Stanisław Barańczak (Ecco, 2016). Reprinted by permission of HarperCollins.

James Tate, 'Pride's Crossing', from *Selected Poems* (Wesleyan University Press, 1991).

Kae Tempest, 'Love', from *Running Upon the Wires* (Picador, 2018). Copyright © Kae Tempest 2018.

Jack Underwood, 'I promise when I lift your egg', from *Happiness* (Faber and Faber Limited).

Dara Wier, 'One Enchanted Evening', from *Voyages in English* (Carnegie Mellon University Press, 2001).

Luke Wright, 'Honeymoon at Weybourne', from *Peak* (Nasty Little Press, 2023).

Tiphanie Yanique, 'Traditional Virgin Islands Wedding Verse', from *Wife* (Peepal Tree Press, 2015).

Adam Zagajewski, 'Transformation', from *Without End: New and Selected Poems*, trans. Clare Cavanagh (Farrar Straus & Giroux, 2002).